Can you find the architect hiding in each building?

To Dad, my favourite building inspector – RD

To my daughter Chloe, the love of my life, and to the amazing team at Phaidon – Maya, Rachel and Meagan – who have guided and inspired me to grow as an artist – JC

Written in consultation with Professor Naomi Stead, architectural critic and scholar at RMIT Melbourne.

About the author

Rebecca Donnelly is the author of over thirty children's books, including *Total Garbage: A Messy Dive into Trash, Waste, and Our World* and *We Spy Fungi: Search and Find Mushrooms, Cacti, and Other Fascinating Plants*. She loves to learn about interesting things and explain them to young readers. For this book, she visited all sorts of buildings and even went behind the scenes in a museum!

About the illustrator

Jocelyn Cho is a San Francisco–based illustrator whose work spans a diverse range of publications, including magazines, school textbooks and fiction book covers. She loves spending her free time exploring indie bookshops, antique shops and museum stores. The details in the buildings featured in this book are inspired by memories of places she visited in her childhood and during her travels around the world.

Phaidon Press Limited
2 Cooperage Yard
London E15 2QR

Phaidon Press Inc.
111 Broadway
New York, NY 10006

Phaidon SARL
55, rue Traversière
75012 Paris

phaidon.com

First published 2025
© 2025 Phaidon Press Limited
Text © Rebecca Donnelly 2025
Illustrations © Jocelyn Cho 2025

Artwork drawn and painted digitally

ISBN 978 1 83729 021 5 (UK edition)
002-0725

A CIP catalogue record for this book is available from the British Library.

All rights reserved. No part of this publication may be reproduced, stored in a retrieval system or transmitted, in any form or by any means, electronic, mechanical, photocopying, recording or otherwise, without the written permission of Phaidon Press Limited.

Printed in China

Commissioning Editor: Maya Gartner
Project Editor: Rachel Craig-McFeely
Production Controller: Rebecca Price
Design: Meagan Bennett

What's That Building?

An Architectural Guessing Game

Words by Rebecca Donnelly
Pictures by Jocelyn Cho

Building knowledge!

Have you ever wondered why buildings look the way they do?

Buildings look different because we use them for different things.

Why do airports have lots of large windows, but planetariums have none? Why do aquariums have tanks, but schools have classrooms?

When we go to a cinema, we want to sit down, watch an exciting film and maybe eat something yummy – so a cinema needs comfy seats, big screens and a popcorn machine!

Someone who designs buildings is called an architect. Architects have a lot to think about: who will use this building, and how will they use it? Designing a building is a bit like solving a puzzle!

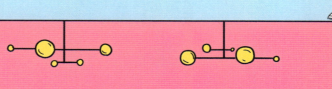

YOU can solve puzzles, too.

There are ten mystery buildings in this book. Can you guess what they are?

Each has clues about who uses the building and what it's used for.

Turn the page for the answer. You can take a closer look at the building and all the busy people inside. What do you think makes the building special?

It's time to guess that building – let's go!

You can find the words in **bold** in the glossary.

If you need space for...

Learning about maths, history, art, music and lots more!

Students and teachers.

Playing and running around.

Lots of rooms, with easy ways to get to them.

Teaching supplies, from books, to instruments, to microscopes.

What building do you need?

A school!

A school is a building where teachers help students learn, play and make friends. It needs space for all sorts of activities, from playing sport to doing science experiments, from eating lunch to reading quietly.

What do you think makes a school a good place to learn and play?

A school has lots of classrooms. Classrooms have desks and chairs for all the students. Digital screens are for showing lessons and looking up information. There are shelves for books and cabinets for stationery. Some classrooms are for specific subjects. Can you spot the science **laboratory** and the art room?

A school has lots of offices. The school receptionist greets students and visitors in the main office. The nurse's office has drawers and cabinets with first aid supplies. If you don't feel well, this is the place to go! Which office do you think the headteacher works in?

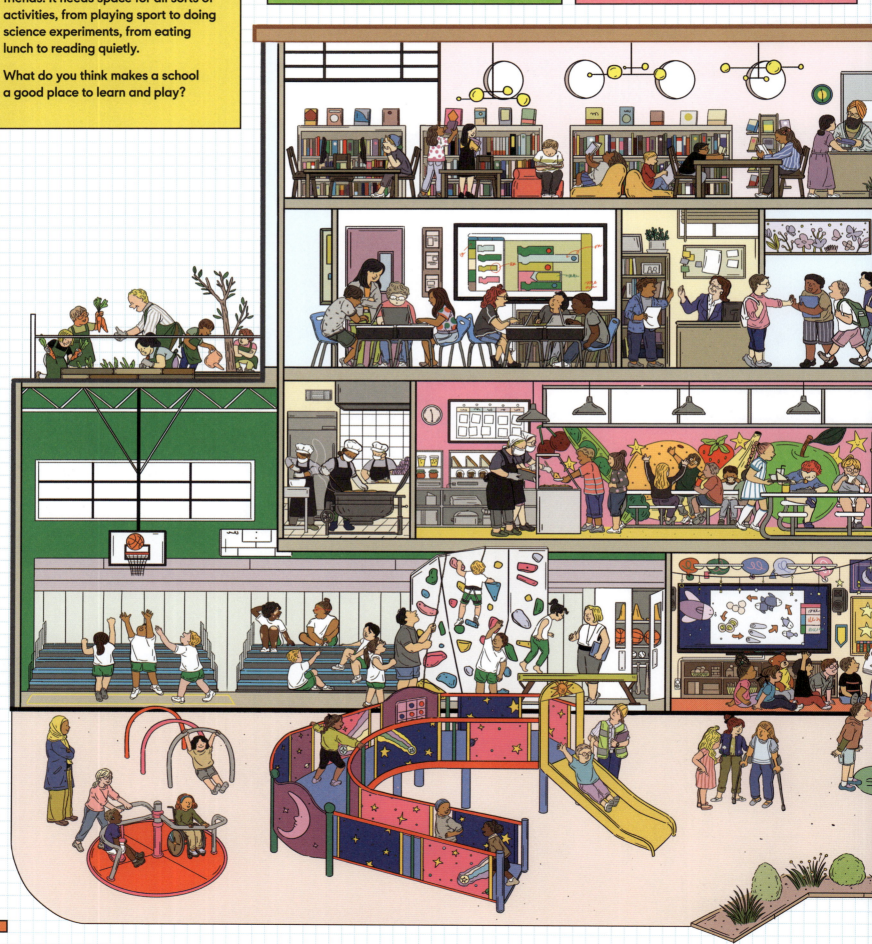

A school has spaces to be active outdoors.
The playground is a place to climb, swing, run and play. It has equipment to help all students use their bodies in different ways and join in the fun. There is a grassy space for playing team sports such as football. Look, someone is about to score a goal!

A school has spaces to be active indoors.
The gym needs a lot of floor space so that students can run, jump, hop, throw, catch, balance and sometimes stand still! People can sit on the benches when they're watching a match.

A school has a canteen.
The canteen is like a big restaurant. Students eat their lunches in the canteen, and the staff cook food in the kitchen. They have to make lots of food! The hot food goes in steam trays to stay warm. Food that needs to stay cold goes in refrigerated cases. What do you like to have for lunch?

Can you find me?

If you need space for...

Small things, like insects.

Big things, like dinosaur bones.

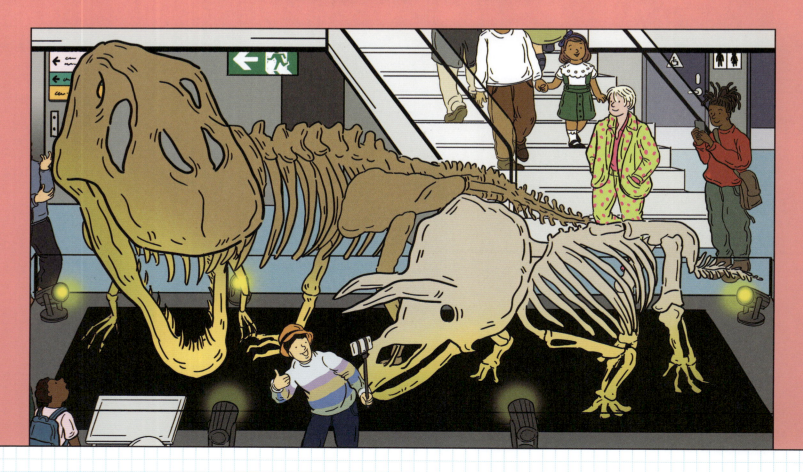

Fixing and saving delicate objects.

Listening, touching and exploring.

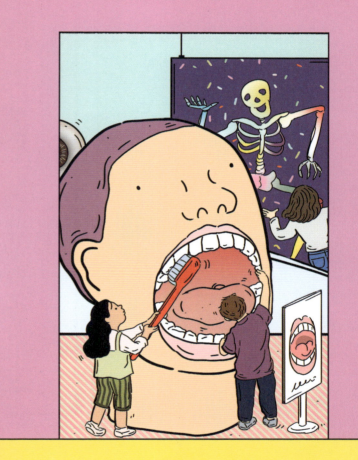

Learning about the past and the future.

What building do you need?

A museum!

A museum is a place that collects, organizes and displays objects for people to see and discover. In a science museum, you can learn about all sorts of interesting things, from dinosaurs to how the human body works!

What makes a museum exciting to explore?

A museum has signs with information. You might need help deciding what to see. Signs direct people up and down stairs and **lifts**, and through doorways and hallways to see all the different items on show. Where do you want to go first?

A museum has displays and exhibits. Museum displays are full of information. Models show you what happens inside the human body or deep down in the soil. There are small cases for small objects and large cases for large objects. The dinosaur skeletons are too big to fit in any case! Together, the objects in each room tell a story. What is each room saying?

A museum has things to touch and do. In some museums, you have to keep your hands to yourself. Here, there are plenty of things you can touch. Interactive screens let you control lights, sounds and more. Some displays let you build models, play games or even climb inside.

A museum has secret rooms. Visitors only see part of what's inside a museum. The museum staff knows all the secrets. Can you spot the sign that shows that visitors aren't allowed? In this hidden room, scientists study bones that are kept in special drawers to keep them safe. Sleep tight, bones!

A museum has controlled conditions. Some objects in a museum need special treatment as direct sunlight, **humidity** and heat can damage them. Many of the windows in a museum have a clever covering that **filters** out daylight. There are also systems to keep the air from getting too dry or too moist. Heating and cooling systems keep the temperature just right.

If you need space for...

Travelling to a different galaxy!

Sitting down while looking up.

Watching videos about space and science.

Learning about stars and planets.

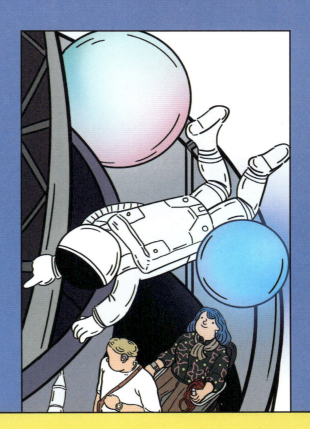

Stargazers of all ages.

What building do you need?

A planetarium!

A planetarium is like a cinema, but it has one special purpose: it's built to teach you about space. Settle back in your chair and look up. Some chairs tilt back to give you an even better view! You might see the planets in our solar system or stars far out in space.

What do you think makes a planetarium the perfect place to see the night sky?

Can you find me?

A planetarium has a curved ceiling.
The ceiling of a planetarium is shaped like a **dome** and the chairs inside are placed in a semicircle. When you're sitting down, you can see all around you. The dome is made of curved steel and covered by aluminium **panels**. The panels are coated with special paint that lets the inside of the dome become a cinema screen.

A planetarium has projectors.
A projector is a piece of equipment that uses light to show a picture or a video on a screen. The projectors in a planetarium can show all sorts of things, from the starry night sky to videos about space travel and science. Which planets and stars would you like to see?

A planetarium is dark.
To use a projector, you need darkness. That's why there are no windows in a planetarium. But it's not completely dark – you don't want to bump into things! Dim lights around the edge of the room help you find your seat.

A planetarium has speakers.
The speakers are hidden behind the dome screen. Millions of tiny holes in the ceiling panels let sound come through. The sound bounces against the dome and comes back to you, so you can hear all the speakers perfectly. The sound system also helps you hear what the presenter is saying.

A planetarium has an air flow system.
There is no air in space, but every building on Earth needs good air flow – otherwise, you wouldn't be able to breathe! In a planetarium, cool air comes through small holes in the ceiling panels. The show can make you feel like you're whizzing through space, and that makes some people feel ill. Cool air helps motion sickness go away.

If you need space for...

Hundreds of shoppers!

Fun things to do.

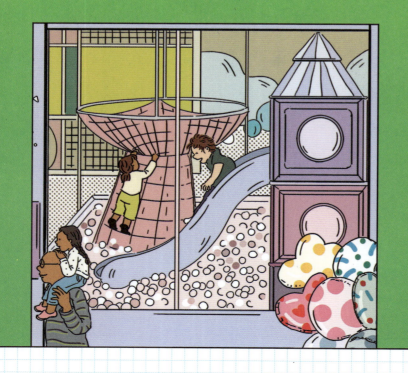

Looking at things to buy.

Moving easily from one shop to the next.

Getting a bite to eat... and maybe watching a film.

What building do you need?

A shopping centre!

This shopping centre has so many things to do, you could spend all day there shopping, playing, eating and watching films.

What makes a shopping centre a fun place to spend time?

A shopping centre has lots of shops. There are shoe shops, bookshops and toy shops. There are big shops and small shops. You can buy things to wear and things to decorate your home. What do you want to buy?

A shopping centre has open spaces. There are so many people in a shopping centre! Some walk slowly, some walk quickly and some use mobility aids such as wheelchairs. Spaces are wide so that everyone can get where they want to go. There are **escalators** and **lifts** to help people go between floors easily.

A shopping centre has lots of signs. Signs show people where to go. Can you spot some in the picture? There are signs for all the shops, signs for toilets, and signs for places to eat and have fun. When it's time to go, follow the sign to the car park.

A shopping centre has windows inside. The windows of a building are usually on the outside – to let in light – but most of the windows in a shopping centre are on the inside! You can look in the windows to see what's for sale in all the different shops.

A shopping centre has spaces to rest. Are you tired yet? There are benches in shopping centres where people can sit to rest or wait. Are you hungry or thirsty? Shopping centres also have cafés and restaurants.

Can you find me?

If you need space for...

Baking bread and cakes.

Keeping ingredients cold.

Mixing batter and kneading dough.

Displaying yummy things to eat.

Sitting and enjoying treats!

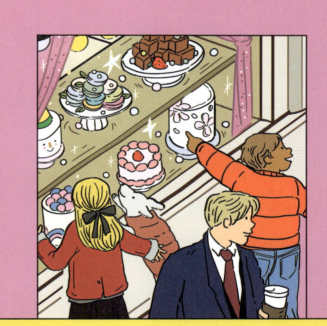

What building do you need?

A bakery!

Can you find me?

So much happens in a bakery! Bakers start their day early, measuring and mixing ingredients in the kitchen. Dough rises. Cakes are baked and decorated. Customers come into the bakery to buy delicious treats.

What makes a bakery a good place to bake and eat?

A bakery is clean and safe.
It has sinks for the bakers to wash their hands and large dishwashers to clean bowls, trays and other tools. The floors in a bakery might get wet and messy, so **textured** surfaces make them less slippery. A bakery has shelves and cabinets to keep things organized.

A bakery has big machines.
Some of the work in a bakery is done by machines. Massive mixers combine ingredients into batches of batter and dough. Rolling machines flatten biscuit dough. Bakery machines can make thousands of biscuits every week. How many biscuits could you eat?

A bakery has refrigerators.
Refrigerators in a bakery are so big that you can walk right into them! A blast cooler chills warm cakes and biscuits fresh from the oven to make them easier to decorate. Bakers get hot, too! **Air conditioning** cools the bakers down.

A bakery has ovens for baking.
Bakery ovens aren't like your oven at home. They're much bigger, and they can get much hotter. This bakery has a rack oven. Rack ovens are tall and have space for lots of trays at once. Some bakeries have long tunnel ovens. Baked goods travel through the oven and come out the other side, like a car driving through a tunnel!

A bakery has space to display treats.
In the back of a bakery, people work hard to make tasty baked goods. In the front of a bakery, the treats go on display for customers to buy. Big glass cases show off all the yummy things for sale. Customers can sit at the tables in the café to enjoy their food. What would you like to eat?

If you need space for...

Shopping and eating while waiting for your flight.

Sitting – or maybe snoozing – during long waits.

Watching aeroplanes take off and land.

Transporting luggage from one place to another.

Passengers, pilots and air traffic controllers.

What building do you need?

An airport!

An airport is a place where people go to catch a flight on an aeroplane. Some people are visiting family and others are going on holiday.

What makes an airport a good place to start an adventure?

An airport has terminals.
The buildings where you prepare to get on or off a flight are called terminals. Screens show you when flights are arriving and departing. Waiting doesn't have to be boring! You can visit a shop or eat at a restaurant. There are also lots of seats – some people try to nap.

An airport has ways to move luggage.
Your luggage travels, too! Suitcases ride on **conveyor belts** through the airport and out on to the **tarmac**, ready to be loaded into the aeroplane. When you reach your destination, they do the same thing in reverse. Your luggage then goes round and round on the **baggage carousel**. Grab it before it gets away!

An airport has security systems.
Before you can get on an aeroplane, security agents check your ticket and passport. They also make sure that no one is carrying anything dangerous. Your bag goes through the scanner so that agents can see what's inside, and you get scanned in an even bigger machine.

An airport has ways to get around.
Quick! To help you get to your flight on time, moving sidewalks speed you through the terminal. **Escalators** and **lifts** move between floors. Some airports are so huge, a special train takes you from one part to another.

An airport has hangars and towers.
Aeroplanes are built to fly – but sometimes they need to take a rest! An aircraft hangar is a huge building where aeroplanes go for inspections and repairs. The tall communication tower is where air traffic controllers make sure all the aeroplanes take off and land safely. All clear!

Can you find me?

If you need space for…

Lots of different types of food, from fruit to chocolate.

Shopping trolleys and baskets.

Keeping cold foods cool.

Packing up groceries and paying for them.

Organizing all the food and supplies.

What building do you need?

A supermarket!

People go to a supermarket to buy food, as well as lots of other useful things. There are thousands of different items on the shelves.

What do you think makes a supermarket a useful place to shop?

A supermarket is organized.
Different items go in different areas in a supermarket. Signs in each section show you where to find what you're looking for. There are **aisles** of shelves, refrigerators and freezers, as well as counters for meat, fish, baked goods and prepared food.

A supermarket has lots of shelves.
Rows of long, tall shelves store food and other things that don't need to stay cold. Similar items go together – boxes of crackers in one section, tins of soup in another. The aisles are wide so people can push trolleys easily.

A supermarket keeps food fresh.
Foods that need to stay cold go in refrigerators and freezers. The doors are made of glass so you can see what's inside. Fresh fish is kept on ice at the fish counter. Fruits and vegetables go in the produce section near the entrance.

A supermarket has secret places.
Before your food get on to the shelf, it arrives inside large lorries. Everything is unloaded and stored in the back of the supermarket. Supermarket workers put the products on the shelves. Workers also bake cakes, slice meat and make salads in the back of the shop. Next time you see a supermarket worker, say thank you!

A supermarket has shopping trolleys.
Pick up a trolley or basket on your way in to carry your items. When you're ready to pay, go to the checkout lane. Here, a **conveyor belt** moves your shopping to a supermarket worker, who scans your items and tells you how much you need to pay. Now it's time to go home.

If you need space for...

Waiting for an appointment.

Letting sick animals rest and get better.

Examining pets to make sure they're healthy.

Pet supplies and medical equipment.

Doing surgery for animals that need it.

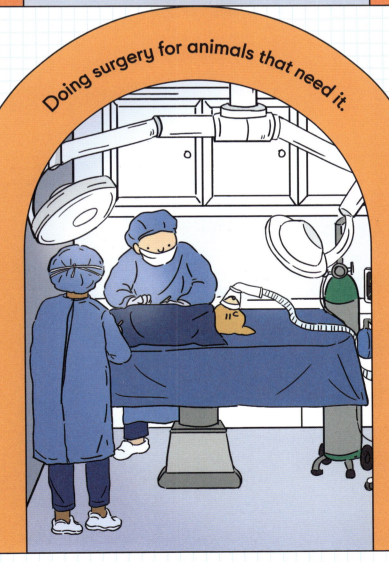

What building do you need?

A veterinary clinic!

Do you have a pet? Pets go to the veterinary (vet) clinic for checkups and to help them feel better when they're ill. Wild animals can also be brought here if they're unwell.

What do you think makes a vet clinic a good place to take care of animals?

A vet clinic has a reception area. This is where you and your pet wait before you see the vet (a doctor for animals). The receptionist checks you in and makes appointments.

A vet clinic is clean. Everything needs to stay clean in a vet clinic. You don't want germs to spread! **Air conditioning** machines **filter** the air. A machine called an autoclave cleans tools. There is a laundry room for washing blankets, and space to store clean uniforms for the staff.

A vet clinic has examination rooms. The vet checks that pets are healthy in an examination room. There are scales for weighing, and the vet has tools for looking inside and listening to your pet's body. The examination tables are made of metal. It's easy to clean and hard for pets to scratch!

A vet clinic has medical equipment. Sometimes, pets need special medical care. A vet uses X-ray machines and ultrasound machines to take pictures of your pet's bones and organs. The walls of the X-ray room are thick because X-rays can be dangerous. If needed, pets get surgery in the operating room.

A vet clinic has comfy beds for pets. Do you like to rest when you're ill? Steel kennels are safe, comfy places for pets to recover after treatment. Kennels also keep pets apart so they don't accidentally make each other ill. Feel better soon, pets!

If you need space for...

Taking care of fish, rays, turtles and more!

Learning about sea life.

Lots and lots of water.

Homes for underwater animals.

Watching underwater creatures swim, eat and play.

What building do you need?

An aquarium!

An aquarium is a place where people go to learn about underwater plants and animals. Lots of animals live in aquariums – mermaids don't actually live here, though! Aquarium designers and staff work hard to make sure aquarium tanks are as close as possible to how animals live in the wild.

What makes an aquarium a good place to care for underwater life?

An aquarium has lots of tanks.
Aquarium tanks are see-through, so you can watch the animals that live in them. Tanks are made from very strong plastic, not glass. To be strong enough to hold all the water, a glass window would be so thick you couldn't see through it!

An aquarium has lots of clean water.
Underwater animals and plants need clean, healthy water. The water in an aquarium tank goes through a system of pipes, tanks, pumps and filters to take out sand and animal poo! Animals that come from the sea have salt added to their water. Large aquariums can **filter** millions of litres of water every day.

An aquarium has airflow systems.
Some animals, such as fish, breathe underwater. The water in an aquarium tank needs the right amount of oxygen. Devices called **aerators** take away the carbon dioxide that animals breathe out and add oxygen for them to breathe in.

An aquarium has kitchens.
Animals in an aquarium need to eat many different types of food, such as small fish, krill and plankton. The animals' food is stored and prepared in a kitchen. Some aquariums have vegetable gardens to feed turtles and other plant eaters, while some even grow aquatic plants such as seaweed. Can you see the different ways the animals are being fed?

An aquarium has exhibits and laboratories.
Aquariums have displays and signs that teach people how to keep underwater animals and plants safe. You can even interact with creatures up close at the touch tank! Aquariums are also places where scientists learn more about sea life – can you spot the **laboratory** where scientists are researching coral?

Can you find me?

If you need space for...

Displaying books for readers to find.

Comfy places to read.

Listening to stories.

Quiet places to work and study.

Playing and having fun!

What building do you need?

A library!

Libraries are buildings that keep books for local people to borrow. You can sit and read, or go to a craft session or story time.

What do you think makes a library a good place to read and have fun?

A library has strong floors.
Libraries have thousands of books. Some have hundreds of thousands! The shelves and floors have to be very strong to hold so many books. A library with more than one **storey** needs very strong walls and supports such as thick columns.

A library is organized.
As well as books, libraries also have films, magazines and music. Shelving and signs make it easy to find what you're looking for. Some books are organized by their subject, and some by the author's last name. Do you organize your books at home?

A library has electricity and lights.
There are lots of plug sockets for people to plug in their electronic devices. There are also plenty of lights, and windows to let in the sun. Light brightens up the library. It's tricky to read in the dark!

A library has spaces to gather.
Libraries are places for everyone in the community. There are different rooms for different activities. There are rooms for story time and classes, and rooms for quiet working. Libraries can be noisy, too! Walls keep loud sounds from drifting into quiet areas.

A library has a place just for you!
Some libraries have toys, tables to do crafts, and a rug to sit on to listen to stories. The children's area has low shelves to make it easy for you to reach books. You can get lots of ideas at the library! It's okay if some of those ideas escape – can you spot them?

You can be an architect, too!

Look around where you live.
What buildings can you see?

You might spot the same kinds of buildings you've seen in this book – and plenty of different ones, too.

What kind of building would you like to design?

What would it look like?

Who will use it?

What features would it need?

The most important tool every architect needs is their imagination.

Buildings can be as creative and unique as the people who build them – and the people who use them!

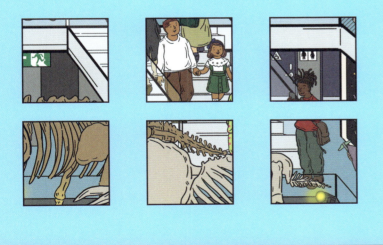

Glossary of architectural words

Use these words to talk about buildings!

aerator: A piece of equipment that provides a supply of air, for example, to water.

air conditioning: A system used to cool down the air inside a building.

aisle: An indoor walkway.

baggage carousel: A conveyor belt that moves in a circle, where people pick up their luggage after a flight.

conveyor belt: A mechanical device that moves items using a continuously moving loop of material.

dome: A round roof or ceiling.

escalator: A moving staircase that takes people from one storey to another inside a building.

filter: To remove unwanted substances, for example, from air, light or water.

humidity: How much water there is in the air.

laboratory: A place where people carry out science experiments.

lift: A machine that lifts and lowers people and things inside a building.

panel: A piece of material that forms one section of a surface.

storey: A floor of a building.

tarmac: A material used to make road surfaces and airport runways.

textured: Something that is not smooth.

 Cardiff Libraries
www.cardiff.gov.uk/libraries

Llyfrgelloedd Caerdydd
www.caerdydd.gov.uk/llyfrgelloedd

ACC. No: 07039855

NATURAL WONDERS OF THE WORLD

MOLLY OLDFIELD

Illustrated by
FEDERICA BORDONI

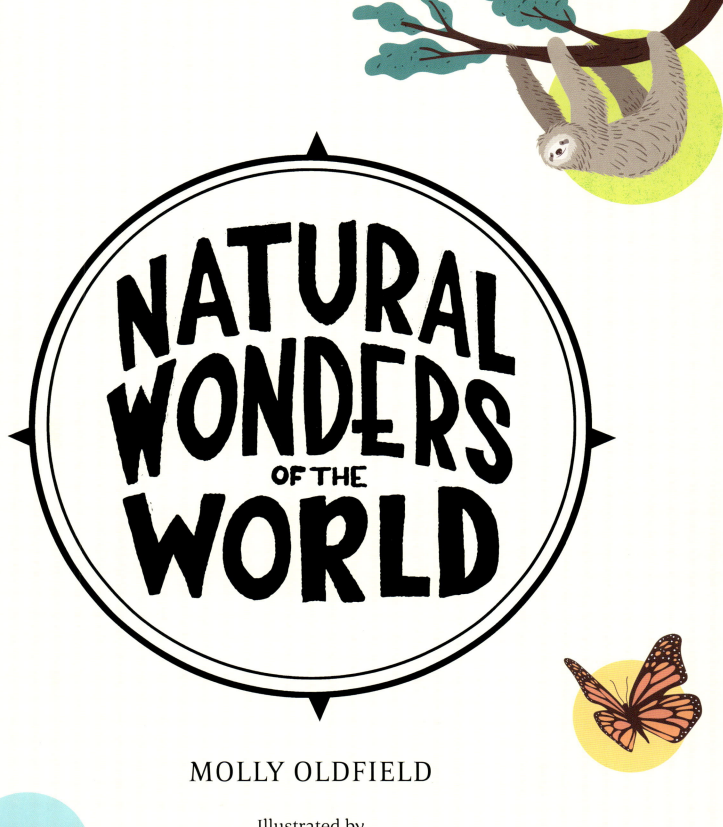

wren
&rook

CONTENTS

- **4. INTRODUCTION**
- **6. CAVE OF GIANTS**
  Fingal's Cave, Scotland
- **8. THE SHOW-OFFS**
  Birds of Paradise, New Guinea
- **10. EARTH MEETS SKY**
  Salar de Uyuni, Bolivia
- **12. THE ISLANDS OF SCI-FI**
  Socotra Archipelago, Yemen
- **14. PENGUIN CENTRAL**
  Zavodovski Island, South Sandwich Islands
- **16. CURTAINS OF LIGHT**
  Aurora Borealis, The North
- **18. VOLCANIC WILDERNESS**
  Yellowstone National Park, USA
- **20. GLEAMING SHARDS**
  Cave of Crystals, Mexico
- **22. WET AND DRY**
  Namib Desert, Angola, Namibia and South Africa
- **24. COASTAL INVADERS**
  Christmas Island Crabs, Christmas Island; Firefly Squid, Japan
- **26. NATURE'S CRADLE**
  Ngorongoro Crater, Tanzania
- **28. ISLAND OF ROCK**
  Uluru, Australia
- **30. SAFE HAVEN**
  Seal Island, South Africa
- **32. HEIGHTS OF GRANDEUR**
  Giant Forest, USA

34. ONE OF A KIND
Animals of Madagascar, Madagascar

36. DEVIL'S THROAT
Iguazú Falls, Argentina and Brazil

38. SCARLET WATERS
Lake Natron, Tanzania

40. LUNGS OF THE PLANET
Amazon Basin, South America

42. TORTOISE SANCTUARY
Aldabra, Seychelles

44. A RIVER MAKES ITS MARK
Grand Canyon, USA

46. RAINFOREST OF THE OCEAN
Great Barrier Reef, Australia

48. EVERLASTING STORM
Catatumbo lightning, Venezuela

50. LAND OF THE ICE GIANTS
Eisriesenwelt, Austria

52. THE FLUTTER OF 200 MILLION WINGS
Monarch butterfly migration, North America

54. TRAIL OF BLOSSOM
Sakura Zensen, Japan

56. PREHISTORIC FOREST
Gondwana Rainforests, Australia

58. THE EYE OF THE SEA
Great Blue Hole, Belize

60. GLOWING CAVES
Waitomo Caves, New Zealand

62. INDEX

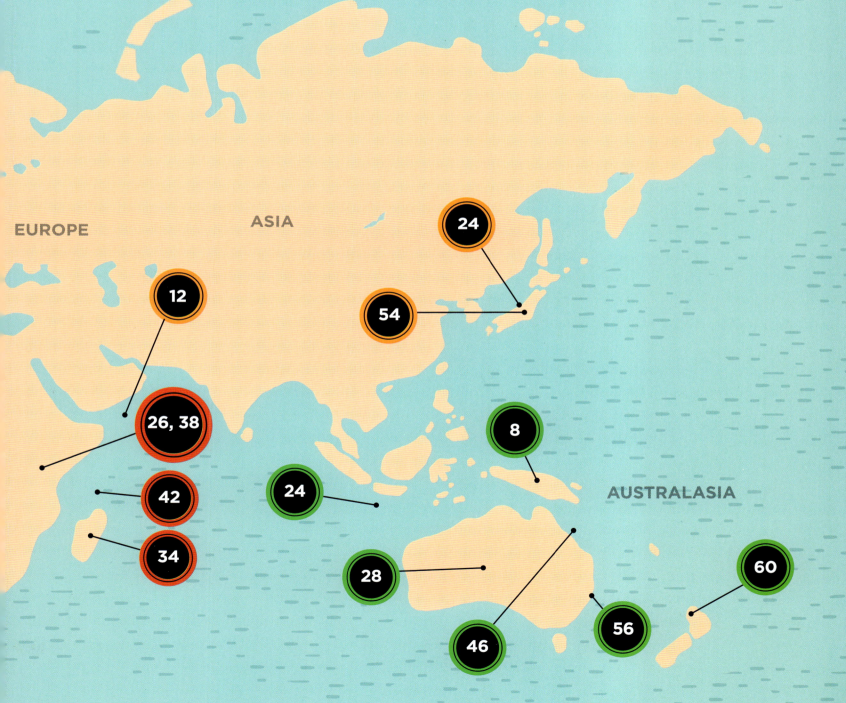

We live on the most beautiful planet. Our natural world is filled with fascinating animals, majestic trees and beautiful flowers, all living in epic landscapes from glittering coral reefs to mighty snow-capped mountains, and from lush rainforests to dry windswept deserts. How lucky we are to live here!

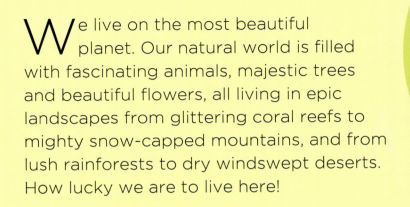

INTRODUCTION
MOLLY OLDFIELD

I love to travel and explore. I wanted to create a book that is like a passport to the world, filled with pages that take you to the most incredible natural wonders on Earth. Get ready for adventures!

Swing through the trees of the island of Madagascar, waving at lemurs, aye-ayes and tenrecs as you pass. Dive into the ocean to explore the Great Barrier Reef, the world's largest living organism. Delve into a sea cave said to be built by a giant. Stand in the most electric place on Earth.

You will discover plenty of animals too: birds of paradise with exquisite colourful feathers, butterflies that fly thousands of kilometres in search of the Sun, and giant tortoises that live on remote tropical islands. You'll uncover incredible plants like dragon's blood trees and giant sequoias, the largest trees in the world.

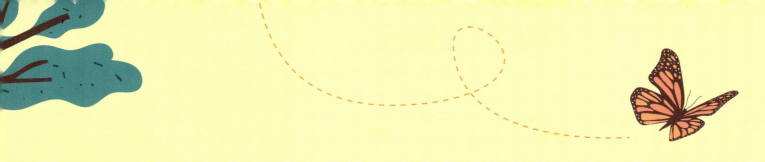

There is something for everyone in this collection; think of it like a map of the most amazing natural creations on Earth. One day you might visit some of these places (perhaps you already have!). If not, don't worry; you can discover them by reading about them in your favourite spot – be that curled up in an armchair, or in the branches of a tree.

Of course, don't forget that wonders can be found much closer to home, too – all you need to do to experience the natural world is step outside. In your neighbourhood you'll find beautiful trees, blossom and animals, not to mention skies filled with sunshine, thunderclouds and sparkling stars.

As well as showing you the majesty and variety of life on Earth, I hope this book will remind you how fragile and precious our planet really is. Many of the world's natural wonders are in danger thanks to global warming. Humans are threatening our planet by burning fossil fuels – like coal and wood – to create energy to power homes, cars, planes and factories. When these fuels are burned, they release carbon dioxide into the atmosphere, heating up the planet so much that many of the natural wonders in this book are being damaged.

There are lots of people working on ways to reduce our carbon dioxide emissions, such as by using recyclable materials to build things we need and by harnessing nature to produce renewable solar and wind energy. But there's lots more to do – perhaps you will come up with a new idea to protect the Earth someday!

In the meantime, there are many ways you can help. You could travel by public transport rather than by car (or best of all, cycle or walk!), recycle as much as possible, try to cut down on plastic and grow your own vegetables. Everything helps, and each small act adds up to make a difference.

I hope this book shows you the richness of the world and the variety of life on Planet Earth. It's our great fortune that we live here, so let's take care of it and delight in it. Turn the pages of this book and set off on a journey to fill your life with these wonders of the natural world …

Fingal's Cave, on the uninhabited Scottish island of Staffa, looks so fantastical that legends have grown up around it. Ancient people thought that something so majestic could only have been built by a giant …

CAVE OF GIANTS
FINGAL'S CAVE, SCOTLAND

As the story goes, the giant was named Finn McCool. He was 16-m tall, and he lived in Ireland with his wife Oonagh. One day, he heard there was a rival giant in Scotland called Benandonner and challenged him to a fight. He built a bridge of stepping-stones made out of hexagonal rocks to take him over the sea to Scotland. When Finn crossed the bridge, he saw that his rival was much bigger than he was and ran home afraid. With the Scottish giant close behind, Finn's quick-thinking wife dressed him up as a baby. When Benandonner saw him, he thought, *Well, if Finn's baby is THIS big, just imagine how huge he must be!* Benandonner rushed back to Scotland, ripping up the bridge as he went. Now all that's left is the beginning and the end: an incredible rock formation in Ireland, called the Giant's Causeway, and Fingal's Cave in Scotland.

Of course, these two wonders weren't really built by a giant, but they were both created at the same time in history: an underground volcano erupted some 65 million years ago and caused the basalt rock in both places to crack and re-form in amazing hexagonal columns.

Beautiful sounds are created by the sea in the cave. In fact, German composer Felix Mendelssohn once sailed to Fingal's Cave and was inspired by the magnificent echo of the smashing waves. See if you can find his piece called *Fingal's Cave* online. Can you hear the waves crashing?

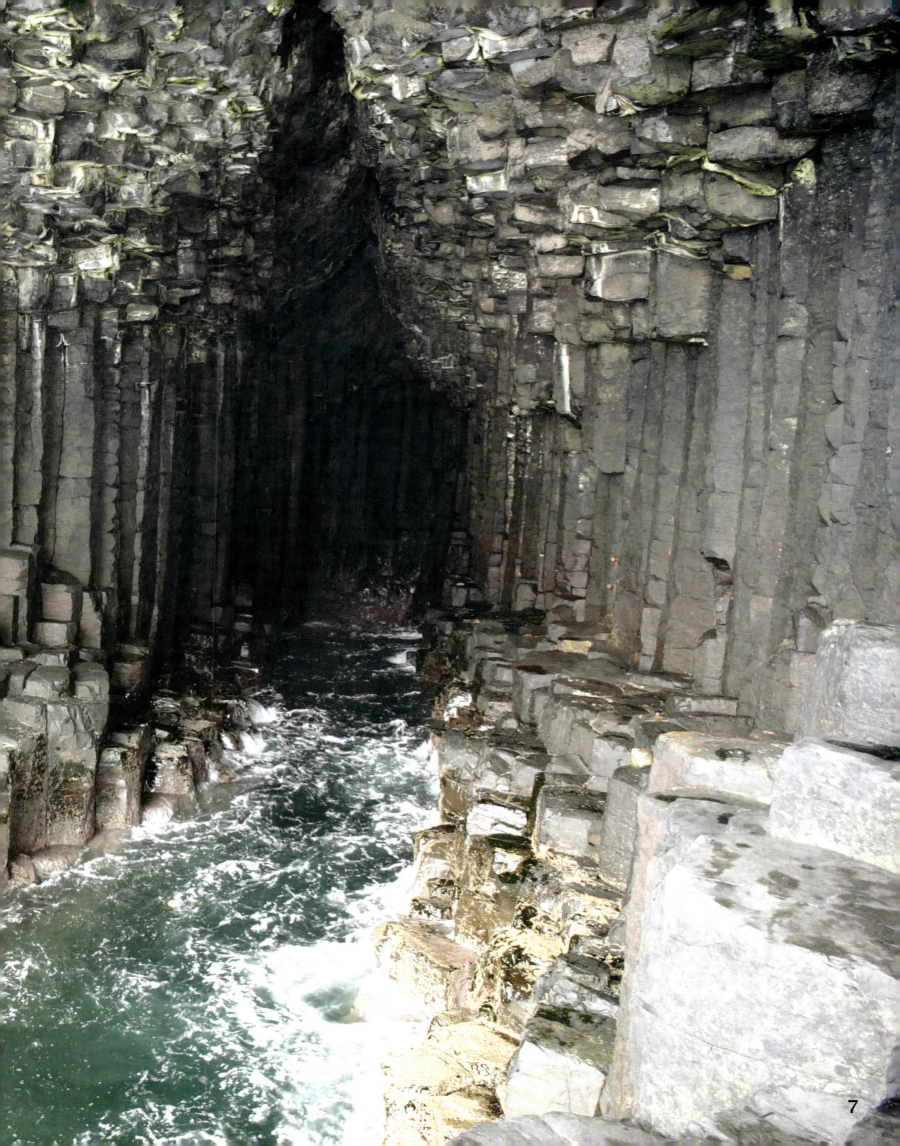

If you ever visit the jungle-covered island of New Guinea in the Pacific Ocean, you'll be in for a treat. With feathers as bright as jewels, unusual songs and skilful dance moves, male birds of paradise are perhaps the most spectacular birds on Earth.

THE SHOW-OFFS
BIRDS OF PARADISE, NEW GUINEA

There are 43 species of birds of paradise. The females look rather drab, but they are *very* picky about which males they will breed with. That's because there isn't much competition for food on New Guinea. Since the females can easily find enough food for themselves and their chicks, they don't need a male to help out.

As a result, over millions of years of evolution, the males have had to become really impressive to compete against one another. The more exquisite they look and the more they can show off, the greater chance they have of a female noticing them, so male birds of paradise have beautiful feathers and plumes.

Each of the males also has a unique display to attract a female, made up of exciting wiggles, jumps, dances and feather movements, as well as unusual songs. Some dance on branches; others dance on poles they make themselves, polishing them with a little leaf to make a perfect stage; some dance alone; others dance in groups.

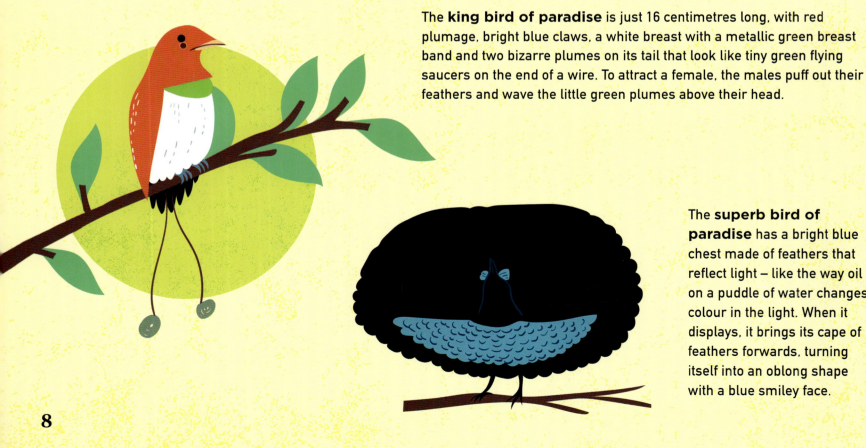

The **king bird of paradise** is just 16 centimetres long, with red plumage, bright blue claws, a white breast with a metallic green breast band and two bizarre plumes on its tail that look like tiny green flying saucers on the end of a wire. To attract a female, the males puff out their feathers and wave the little green plumes above their head.

The **superb bird of paradise** has a bright blue chest made of feathers that reflect light – like the way oil on a puddle of water changes colour in the light. When it displays, it brings its cape of feathers forwards, turning itself into an oblong shape with a blue smiley face.

The largest sub-species is the **greater bird of paradise**, which is 43 cm long, maroon brown in colour, with a yellow head, green throat and bright yellow feathers to use when showing off to a female.

EARTH MEETS SKY
SALAR DE UYUNI, BOLIVIA

The Salar de Uyuni is the world's largest salt flat. It is so enormous and piercingly white that Neil Armstrong could see it when he stood on the moon – he thought it was a giant glacier. You can find it very high up in the Andes mountain range in Bolivia, 3,656 metres above the sea.

The Salar is 10,580 square kilometres in size and was once part of a prehistoric salt lake, Lago Minchín. The lake dried up, leaving behind a huge amount of salt – 10 billion tonnes of it – packed into a crust several metres thick.

When you stand on the Salar, the flat stretches in all directions. The salt tends to form into an intricate pattern of hexagons, so the view before you is of white hexagonal tiles that seem to go on forever. In winter, you can drive across it. In summer, the flat becomes a giant puddle, covered with a thin sheet of water, reflecting the sky and turning the landscape into the world's largest mirror. The Earth and the sky mingle together on the Salar de Uyuni.

The salt flat varies in height by less than a metre, despite covering an area the size of Jamaica. In fact, it is so flat that it can be used

for setting altimeters – devices that measure the height of objects very precisely – which orbit the Earth on man-made satellites.

For generations, Bolivians have been scraping the Salar de Uyuni for salt to sell around the world. However, the future of the flat looks set to be different: powering a green revolution. Beneath the salty crust lies a layer of water that contains around 50–70 per cent of the world's lithium sources. Lithium is used to make batteries and will become increasingly valuable if electric cars, which use lithium batteries, continue to rise in popularity. In some ways, this is good news for the planet.

Lithium batteries can be charged by renewable energy, so using them would be much better for the environment than burning fossil fuels that release carbon dioxide for energy. However, it wouldn't be good news for the Salar de Uyuni, because the lithium mining could destroy it.

If you're lucky enough to visit the salt flat while it's still intact, you could stay at the world's only salt hotel – the walls, floors, tables and beds are made from blocks of salt. It may just be the only hotel in the world with a sign saying, 'Please don't lick the walls!'

Socotra is an archipelago, or group, of four islands in the Indian Ocean, 400 km off the coast of Yemen. The islands are covered in huge sandy beaches, but they also look like the set of a science fiction film. That's because Socotra is filled with unique and curious wildlife that lives only on those four islands – you can't find it anywhere else on Earth.

THE ISLANDS OF SCI-FI
SOCOTRA ARCHIPELAGO, YEMEN

The scientific word for plants or animals that only live in one place in the world is 'endemic'. Socotra has 825 plant species, and over a third of them are endemic. The islands of Socotra are some of the oldest on the planet, having been separated from the mainland more than 250 million years ago. Indeed, that's the reason why they are home to so many strangely unique species of plants and animals. They have been isolated for so long that the wildlife there has evolved separately from creatures on the mainland to look unlike anything else on Earth.

The most unusual of Socotra's plants is the dragon's blood tree, pictured right. It looks like a giant green umbrella and is named after the red sap of the tree – called cinnabar – which was once thought to be dragon's blood!

Socotra is sometimes called 'the Galápagos of the Indian Ocean'. The Galápagos are volcanic islands found 1,000 km off the coast of South America, and are also filled with endemic wildlife. When Charles Darwin travelled to Galápagos and saw the unique animals living there, he started to work on his theory of evolution through natural selection.

Darwin's theory argues that individuals in each species vary greatly because of differences in their genes. Those who are most suited to their environment will be more likely to live and have offspring to whom they pass on their stronger genes. Individuals who aren't well adapted, however, are less likely to survive and reproduce, so their genes will not get passed on. This process continues over millions of years, and gradually the overall species evolves to perfectly suit its environment – just as the wildlife on Socotra has done.

Other plants that grow here and nowhere else on Earth include the Socotran desert rose, left, a tree with a bottle-shaped trunk and small pink flowers.

PENGUIN CENTRAL
ZAVODOVSKI ISLAND, SOUTH SANDWICH ISLANDS

Zavodovski Island is one of the largest penguin colonies in the world, and the conditions are harsh. The penguins live on an active volcano and are battered by the wind and waves of the Southern Ocean. Every day, they dive off steep 10-m-tall cliffs in search of fish to feed their family.

Zavodovski Island is one of the South Sandwich Islands. Found off the coast of frozen Antarctica, it is very remote and surrounded by stormy seas. Few humans have ever visited the island and none live there at all.

In theory, Zavodovski Island isn't a bad place for a penguin to live. That's because there are no predators of penguins there, the seas around the island are full of fish to eat and the volcano's warmth helps to melt the snow on the island.

However, it's a tough life in reality. Males and females take it in turns to leap into the ocean to hunt. If they survive the dive and catch some food, they then have to make it home by riding huge waves on to the rocks and clambering up the cliff with fish in their beaks. The expedition is very dangerous; every day, penguins return from the hunt with cuts, bruises and broken legs. It doesn't smell very nice on the island because of the active volcano: place names include Pungent Point and Noxious Bluff!

The 5-km-wide island is home to an astonishing 1.2 million chinstrap penguins, who are named for the curved line of black feathers that look like a strap on their chins, and 180,000 macaroni penguins, who have a tuft of bright yellow hair.

When a hunting penguin returns to the island, it is somehow able to recognise the cry of its own mate among the racket of over 1 million other penguins.

If you go outside at night in the northern areas of Earth – in places such as Iceland, Greenland, Scandinavia, Siberia, Alaska and Canada – you might be lucky enough to see eerily beautiful coloured light shape-shifting across the sky.

These are the Northern Lights, or the *aurora borealis*. They were named by the seventeenth-century astronomer Galileo Galilei after Aurora, the Roman goddess of the dawn, and *boreal*, the Greek word for the wind of the north. They appear close to the North Pole. The Southern Hemisphere has its own lights too, called the Southern Lights or *aurora australis*. Both auroras appear like magic in the dark of the night, in ever-changing shapes of green, purple, pink and blue.

CURTAINS OF LIGHT

AURORA BOREALIS, THE NORTH

They happen because of our Sun. Its enormous energy causes a wind, known as the solar wind, to flow out into space. Earth is protected by a magnetic field thanks to its core of iron. When the solar wind reaches our planet's magnetic field, it is pushed to the North and South poles. At the poles, the wind reacts with oxygen and nitrogen in the atmosphere, creating beautiful light displays.

Sometimes the Northern Lights can be seen further south than usual. This happens when the Sun is really active, spewing out more solar wind than it normally does. It happened in 37 CE. Seneca, a Roman historian, said the Roman Emperor saw a bright red light in the sky. Thinking it was the military post of Ostia on fire, he sent troops of soldiers over to put it out. But when they got there, they saw only a spectacular display of light in the sky: the Northern Lights, reaching as far south as Italy! A similar thing happened in Britain in 1938 – fire brigades were sent to fight a 'fire' at Windsor Castle that time too. In 2014, the Northern Lights lit up skies all over the UK, but thankfully no fire services were called.

If you ever hear that the Northern Lights are likely to appear near you, the best thing to do is to go out into the countryside, far away from city lights, to a place where the sky is very dark; then you're more likely to catch a glimpse of this astonishing wonder.

Yellowstone National Park really is nature showing off: from volcanic springs, mudpots and geysers to wild animals, forests and lakes, it is no wonder it was made into the world's first national park.

VOLCANIC WILDERNESS

YELLOWSTONE NATIONAL PARK, USA

Spanning 8,983 square km of Wyoming, Montana and Idaho, Yellowstone is an awesome spectacle of canyons, rivers, mountain ranges, forests and waterfalls. It's home to grizzly bears, bison and elk. In the 1990s, wolves were reintroduced after they had all been culled. The wolves brought new life to the park, helping overgrazed areas to regenerate by keeping their elk prey moving, and killing coyotes so more rabbits, foxes and weasels survived. Yellowstone sprang back into life: forests grew, and the tree roots slowed the rivers down, so beavers and fish returned. The wolves caused a transformation.

The park sits on top of the largest volcanic system in North America. There is so much molten rock beneath Yellowstone that it could fill the Grand Canyon 11 times over, and 60 per cent of the world's hot springs and geysers are found there. Geysers occur when cold underground rivers meet hot subterranean rocks; the water is heated rapidly and shoots up to the surface where it flies into the air as steam. If you stand by a geyser, watch out. You'll see a little steam at first, and then … whoosh!

The geyser basin area of Yellowstone is a magical landscape filled with steam fountains, bubbling earth, and boiling pools of multi-coloured water. You can find the Grand Prismatic Spring there, which is bigger than a football pitch and deeper than a ten-storey building. Its turquoise waters are ringed with vivid bands of orange, yellow and green – they're caused by bacteria living in the cool water around the spring.

Designated a national park in 1872, Yellowstone inspired the protection of wildernesses around the world. It's easy to see why.

The Cave of Crystals lies deep under the mountains in Chihuahua, Mexico, and is filled with some of the largest crystals ever found on Earth. They shoot off in all directions, making the Cave of Crystals one of the most spectacular underground caverns on the planet. The biggest crystal in the cave is 12 m long and 4 m in diameter!

GLEAMING SHARDS
CAVE OF CRYSTALS, MEXICO

The cave is located 300 m below the surface of the Earth. If you travelled 2 km even further underground, you would find a magma chamber – a big underground pool of liquid rock, usually found beneath volcanoes. This magma chamber heated the water stored in the cave above it, creating the perfect conditions to form gigantic crystals, which has been happening for the past 500,000 years.

Crystals are transparent, naturally occurring mineral materials. They come in all sorts of shapes and sizes: sugar crystals are oblong, while salt crystals are formed like cubes. The crystals in this cave are made of selenite, which is a soft mineral that is easily scratched.

The crystals grew to enormous sizes very slowly over millennia, unseen by mankind in the dark waters of the cave. Their peaceful growth was shattered in 2000 by two brothers who were working in the nearby Naica mine. Their company had pumped water out of the network of caves to make the mining easier. Imagine how the brothers must have felt when, hard at work, they suddenly broke through a wall into a magical space filled with enormous, ancient crystals!

Those crystals are the largest that have ever been found. They're so big that people can walk along them! While the Cave of Crystals has the largest crystals of them all, other caverns are impressive too, such as the Cave of Swords, named for its metre-long crystals. It's likely there are many more caves still to be discovered.

It is dangerously hot in the cave network, with temperatures of up to 58 °C: that's hotter than the highest temperature ever recorded above ground, in Death Valley, USA. Humans can only survive inside it for 10 minutes without protection, so special suits and breathing equipment have been designed so scientists can explore and study the caves. Even with all that kit, people can still only stay in the caves for about half an hour at a time.

Scientists have found extraordinary ancient life forms trapped inside some of the metre-long crystals. In laboratories, they have been able to bring one of the organisms back to life and they discovered that it's not closely related to anything previously found on Earth. Some people think it's possible that the organism came from somewhere else in the solar system. Others argue that this can't be true. What we do know is that the organism lived around 10,000 or 50,000 years ago and somehow managed to survive with no light in the hot, humid and acidic environment of the cave.

In 2017, the mining company stopped working in the area and allowed water to flow back into the Cave of Crystals. Sadly, that means scientists can no longer study the cave. However, left in watery peace once more, the crystals will now start growing again in the deep, dark cave.

It's strange enough to think of a desert that runs along the edge of the ocean, but the Namib is a coastal desert of huge sand dunes and gravel plains that runs along 2,000 km of the south-western coast of the African continent, crossing Namibia, Angola and South Africa. It began forming around 55 million years ago, possibly making it the oldest desert in the world.

WET AND DRY

NAMIB DESERT, ANGOLA, NAMIBIA AND SOUTH AFRICA

The Namib is also very foggy, which is strange to imagine. The fog forms when the cold Atlantic Ocean collides with the dry, warm air of the Namib. Some areas of the desert spend months each year enveloped in this blanket of fog.

The word Namib means 'open space' in the language of the local Nama people, but the stretch of Namib along the coast is often called The Skeleton Coast because it features so many wrecks of ships that lost their way in the fog. Many of the shipwrecks have been completely destroyed by the sun and salty sea air, but a few are still beached in the sand and can be explored up close by visitors.

Surprisingly, the Namib is full of wildlife because the animals which live there have adapted to its environment. For example, Hartmann's mountain zebras have fast-growing hooves to help them walk on rocky terrain and desert elephants can live for days without drinking water. Smaller creatures have also adapted to live in the foggy conditions. The Namib Desert beetle gathers humidity on its body then flips its backside into the air so the water rolls down into its mouth. The web-footed gecko perches on sand dunes in the morning, waiting for the fog to condense into water droplets on its enormous eyes, then it licks the water off its own eyes with its long tongue.

Namibia was the first country in the world to protect the environment in its constitution, setting a great example to other countries. In 2006, five African nations, including Namibia, decided to pool their resources and work on conservation together, tackling wildlife poaching and climate change. They created the Kavango–Zambezi Transfrontier Conservation Area (KAZA) in an area where the international borders of the five countries meet. Their actions will hopefully help their region's incredible wildlife to survive and thrive!

Sometimes creatures get together in such big numbers to breed that they end up overwhelming their environment and creating marvellous scenes. Discover two brightly coloured spectacles that occur once a year at the coast: a red river created by crabs and a bright blue glow created by squid!

COASTAL INVADERS

CHRISTMAS ISLAND CRABS
Christmas Island

If you travel 360 km south of Java, Indonesia, and 2,600 km north-west of Perth, Australia, you will find Christmas Island. Named for the day it was discovered in 1643, it is home to 120 million red land crabs. For most of the year the crabs live in a forest, but at the beginning of the wet season they scurry out of their holes and across the island to spawn in the sea.

For a week, this red tide of millions of crabs moves towards the sea. The males arrive at the beach first and burrow to make nests. When the females arrive, they mate. The males go home to the forest while the females stay for another two weeks to lay their eggs inside the nest.

On the dawn of the high tide in the last lunar quarter of the year, the crabs each release up to 100,000 eggs into the sea. That's a lot of eggs! Then they scuttle back to the forest. As soon as the eggs enter the sea, they hatch into larvae. Over the next month, millions of the larvae are gobbled up by the manta rays and whale sharks that visit Christmas Island during crab mating season, waiting for a feast. But some larvae survive the tricky month and grow into young crabs.

The baby crabs follow in their parents' claw-steps in a shimmering wave of red back up to the forest. There they hide in tree branches and amongst leaves on the forest floor until they become adults four years later – old enough to take part in the coastal invasion themselves.

The people of Christmas Island are careful during the migration. The crabs are ushered towards tunnels called crab grids that go underneath the roads so they don't get squashed. A crab-sized bridge has even been built on one road!

FIREFLY SQUID
Japan

Each spring, millions of firefly squid light up the beach of the Japanese fishing area of Toyama Bay with an electric-blue glow. During the day, the creatures lurk in the deep waters of the bay, but at night, between the months of March and June, they come to the surface to mate.

At the end of the squids' tentacles are organs called photophores that light up with a blue glow. They give off the light in order to blend in with the moonlight shining from above, so predators don't eat them. The glow produced by just one squid is not very bright – not even enough to read this book in the dark – but when the squid group together in tens of thousands, they create a breathtaking display of neon blue. The word to describe organisms that glow like this is 'bioluminescent'.

As you can imagine, people flock to Toyama Bay to see this phenomenon. There is a Firefly Squid Museum so you can study the creatures up close, but the best way to see the light is by boat tour in the middle of the night.

Ngorongoro Crater, in Tanzania, was created two or three million years ago when a supervolcano exploded and collapsed in on itself. The enormous crater sits inside the Great Rift Valley of Africa, which stretches for 6,400 km across east Africa. As well as being one of the most biodiverse places on Earth, it's also known as the cradle of mankind.

The crater covers an area of 8,300 square km and it is home to a spectacular nature reserve, filled with forests, plains, rivers and ponds. Since it's almost completely enclosed by natural walls around 500 m in height, it has formed its own ecosystem with unusual plants including yellow fever trees and huge fig trees.

30,000 animals have made it their home, such as rare black rhinos, leopards, elephants, lions, cheetahs, wildebeest and buffalo. It is

NATURE'S CRADLE
NGORONGORO CRATER, TANZANIA

also a paradise for birds: around 500 species live there, including flamingos, storks, falcons, eagles and ostriches.

The crater is home to the Maasai people, who live alongside the wildlife, herding their cattle. The Maasai named the crater after the noise their cattle's cowbells make: the bells ring with the sound *ngoro ngoro*. Perhaps one of the most amazing things about Ngorongoro is the way that human beings and wild animals live side by side. This has been the case since long before the Maasai arrived 200 years ago. Human beings and our ancestors have lived in the Great Rift Valley for over three million years.

The most famous skeleton found in east Africa is around 3.2 million years old, and is called Lucy. She is the earliest evidence of mankind ever discovered, and we know she walked upright, but spent some time in trees as well. We think it was in the Great Rift Valley that our ancestors learned to walk upright, to leave the forest and to spread across the world.

Rising up out of the dry, flat land of central Australia is a gargantuan rock, called Uluru, that looks like it hails from another planet. It is 348 m high – taller than the Eiffel Tower – and 9.4 km around. It seems to change colour as the light changes. Sometimes it looks brown, but at sunrise and sunset it glows red.

ISLAND OF ROCK
ULURU, AUSTRALIA

So how did it get there? Uluru began to form over 500 million years ago, long before the time of the dinosaurs. Uluru was part of a huge Himalayan-sized mountain range known as the Petermanns, which eroded away over time. Believe it or not, Uluru is made from the sand that eroded from these mountains.

Over time, the centre of Australia – where Uluru is – slowly became an inland sea. The sand that would become Uluru was buried under water, limestone and mud. There was so much pressure on it that it changed from sand into rock. Over millions of years, softer minerals around it eroded away, and the great red rock emerged.

Uluru is red because the iron-bearing minerals within the rock have rusted in the desert air. Amazingly, the enormous mass that we can see is just the top – most of Uluru is still underground, waiting to emerge. Geologists have a name for this kind of rock – they call it an 'inselberg' or 'island mountain'.

For a time, Uluru was known in English as Ayers Rock, named for an Australian civil servant. But in 1985, the land was handed back to the local indigenous people, the Anangu, and their name for the rock, Uluru, was recognised in 1993. The Anangu feel a deep connection to the rock and the land around it. Uluru is central to Anangu creation myths, which are stories of how the world began and how the life on it came into being. Ancestors of the Anangu left laws about how to care for one another, and for the land, written in the rock. These parts of Uluru are deeply sacred.

The Anangu, and other indigenous peoples of Australia, believe that the world was created during the Dreamtime, a period when their spirit ancestors wandered across Australia singing out the name of everything that they saw: birds, animals, plants, rocks, waterholes and even Uluru. Each ancestor created songs about where they travelled, so the routes they used are called songlines. You can't see the songlines, but indigenous people know they are there; they use them to navigate across the landscape. Just as you might be lost without a map or late without a clock, the indigenous people use the songlines to make their way. For them, history is passed on by singing and dancing the songlines.

Tourists used to be allowed to climb all over Uluru, but the Anangu have asked visitors to refrain from this because it goes against their laws. Instead, they invite visitors to learn more about the rock and to understand that Uluru is not just beautiful – it has a deep significance to Anangu culture too.

Seal Island is a long, narrow island off the coast of Cape Town, South Africa. You might be able to guess why it's called Seal Island – and you would probably be right. Around 64,000 Cape fur seals use the small island – only 800 m long and 50 m wide – as their breeding ground. With no humans around, it's a peaceful place to live most of the time. However, once a year, when the population of seals is at its highest, great white sharks arrive and create a circle around the island known as the Ring of Death!

SAFE HAVEN
SEAL ISLAND, SOUTH AFRICA

When the seals swim out to catch fish, the sharks glide beneath them and surge up to attack with their sharp-toothed jaws. The seals fishing in shallower waters are most in danger.

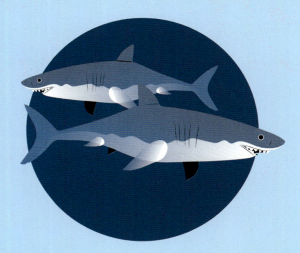

It's possible to visit Seal Island during the shark attack season. Some visitors are even crazy enough to go scuba diving in an underwater cage to get really close to the sharks!

Humans used to be a real threat to Cape fur seals. A century ago, their population was very low because people liked to hunt them for their meat and their furs. Nowadays, it is illegal to hunt seals in South Africa, and there are around two million seals on the shorelines of South Africa and nearby Namibia.

To stand among the trees of the Giant Forest is to feel a part of history. They are ancient: some of these sequoia trees have lived for 3,000 years. Their ancestors have been around for far longer than that – sequoia fossils have been found dating back to when dinosaurs roamed the Earth. Looking up at sunlight filtering through huge branches of majestic sequoias is an awe-inspiring feeling. Their size and age make us seem like tiny specks in the epic history of our planet.

HEIGHTS OF GRANDEUR

GIANT FOREST, USA

Giant Forest is a grove of 8,000 sequoias which grow high on the slopes of the Sierra Nevada mountain range in California, USA. The largest tree on Earth can be found there. Named General Sherman, it is a giant sequoia, standing 83 m tall and measuring 31 m in diameter at the bottom of its trunk – 18 people would have to join arms in order to circle it! In 1978, a branch broke off General Sherman; it was 46 m long and 2 m thick, meaning that just the branch alone was bigger than many other trees are in their entirety. The tree was named after General Sherman, an army general who fought during the American Civil War.

Giant sequoias need almost 2,000 litres of water a day to survive. They get this water from the mountain snow that melts and soaks into the ground in the spring. However, these ancient trees are in danger because of climate change. Less rainfall, decreasing levels of snow, and increasing temperatures all threaten the beautiful giants. Vast forests of giant sequoias used to cover much of the Northern Hemisphere, but now there are very few left – the trees only grow on the small strip of land in the Sierra Nevadas where the Giant Forest is found, among other groves. Each of these giant sequoias is a true wonder; to lose the next generation would be a tragedy.

The island of Madagascar is found in the Indian Ocean, off the coast of Africa. It has been isolated since it broke off from India around 88 million years ago. As a result, the plants and animals on the island evolved independently and have ended up being rather different from creatures and plants in other parts of the world. Like the animals of Socotra, around 80 per cent of the wildlife on Madagascar is endemic: it is found nowhere else in the world.

ONE OF A KIND
ANIMALS OF MADAGASCAR

A **lemur** is a primate that looks like a dog, cat, squirrel and racoon all mixed up. Lemurs come in many shapes and sizes, from the largest of them all, the 10-kg Indri Lemur, which sings across the tree canopy, to the smallest, the pygmy mouse lemur, which weighs just 28 grams. The pygmy mouse lemur hibernates for up to seven months a year, feeding itself on fat stored in its tail.

Aye-ayes are nocturnal primates with huge eyes, big, sensitive ears and long tails. In fact, their tails are as long as their bodies, and they use them to dangle upside down from branches. Aye-ayes find food by tapping on trees with their long, thin middle finger, while listening for little insects moving in the bark. If they find an insect, they scoop it up with the finger and pop it in their mouth. They also use this special finger to scrape flesh out of coconuts and other fruit.

Tenrecs are descendants of small mammals that were washed out to sea from Africa and landed on Madagascar around 40 million years ago. They found themselves with few predators and little competition, so while their cousins in Africa died out, the tenrecs flourished, such as the lowland streaked tenrec, left. They adapted to survive in Madagascar's forests by feeding on insects and other small prey – leading similar lives to those of small mammals and rodents around the world. So tenrecs look like familiar creatures from the mainland because they developed similar traits while living in a similar environment. They can look exactly like mice, shrews and even hedgehogs!

The **hedgehog tenrec** looks like a hedgehog, but isn't one; it's more aggressive than a hedgehog, and hisses, bares its teeth and bucks its head. At night, it rubs its back quills together to make a high-pitched noise that family members can hear, to help them keep close together in the dark forest.

The **web-footed tenrec** looks like a river otter, but isn't one. It lives in water, feeding on frogs, crabs and fish. It sleeps during the day in small streamside burrows. It is incredibly rare and hardly anyone has ever seen one.

Walking amid the thundering Iguazú Falls, the world's largest waterfall system, is a mind-blowing experience. The water is loud, the spray shooting off the falls drenches you, toucans fly above your head and rainbows arc across the sky on a sunny day. The energy, thundering sound and sheer power of the water is completely exhilarating.

DEVIL'S THROAT
IGUAZÚ FALLS, ARGENTINA AND BRAZIL

Iguazú is an indigenous word for 'great water', and indeed, the Iguazú Falls form the largest waterfall system in the world. Around 250 waterfalls, spanning nearly 3 km of the Iguazú river, tumble down to the Parana Plateau, 60–80 m below.

The falls are on the borders of Brazil and Argentina; it is possible to visit the waterfalls in both countries if you have a car or take a taxi over the border. In each country, you'll see a different side to the falls. But the grandest spectacle, at the centre – the largest part of all – is found in Brazil. It's called *la Garganta del Diablo*, which means 'the Devil's Throat' in Spanish.

The waterfalls throw off huge clouds of spray that soak the riverbanks, so a lush, humid and tropical rainforest flourishes around the falls. This rainforest is stuffed with beautiful plants and animals: 2,000 species of plants, 80 tree species and 400 bird species – including the harpy eagle and colourful toucans. Giant anteaters, ocelots, the elusive jaguar and the very rare broad-snouted caiman live around Iguazú.

The area around the falls was made into Iguazú National Park in 1934 for its own protection. It's a good thing too – outside the park, a lot of logging and deforestation goes on. Thank goodness the falls and the rainforest around it are safeguarded for the future, for they really are a majestic sight. Iguazú Falls is truly nature showing off in all her splendour.

Found in Tanzania close to the border with Kenya, the waters of Lake Natron are extremely salty, the temperature of a very hot bath and, most bizarrely of all, bright red!

SCARLET WATERS

LAKE NATRON, TANZANIA

The heat comes from hot springs, the red colour is due to a type of bacteria that lives in the lake and the saltiness is caused by a mineral called sodium carbonate that flows into the lake from the surrounding hills. The mineral is so strongly alkaline – the opposite of acidic – that the Egyptians used it to mummify bodies.

It's a difficult and toxic place to live, so very few creatures have made it their home. However, astonishingly, one bird truly flourishes there: the flamingo! Two million lesser flamingos breed on the lake every year, building nests on islands in the water. The females lay one egg, from which hatches a grey chick the size of a tennis ball. Both parents feed it with a type of milk called crop milk that they regurgitate from their tummies!

Why do flamingos want to live on such a strange lake? It's mostly because of their diet. They feed on an algae called spirulina, which grows in places with lots of alkaline water, such as Lake Natron. Spirulina is full of pigments called carotenoids (also found in things like carrots, egg yolks and autumn leaves), and they eat so much of it that it turns their feathers shades of orange and bubble-gum pink! However, parent flamingos lose their bright pink colour and turn paler – or even white – during the months when they feed their offspring with regurgitated crop milk. Once the chicks start eating on their own, their parents' feathers turn pink again.

Another reason Lake Natron is a good breeding home for the colourful birds is that flamingos have very long legs, which keep their bodies out of the toxic water. That means the flamingos can nest on little islands on the lake, their eggs safe from predators like baboons and wildcats, which can't safely swim through the alkaline waters.

So, although Lake Natron is a terrible spot for most creatures to go for a swim, it is a perfect place for flamingos to lay their eggs – no wonder 75 per cent of the world's lesser flamingos choose to breed their young here.

Flamingo chicks hang out together in groups known as 'crèches', where a few adults take care of them. Parents come and find their own chicks at feeding time.

The Amazon river stretches for 6,800 km from the Andes in Peru, across South America to the Atlantic Ocean in Brazil. It is the largest river in the world by volume. In the wet season, the river's mouth is an astonishing 480 km wide; around 14 million cubic metres of water flow out of the river and into the Atlantic Ocean every day.

More than 1,100 tributaries pour into the Amazon. The river basin drains an area more than twice the size of India, making up the largest river basin on Earth. The Amazon river basin contains forests, savannahs, swamps and the Amazon Rainforest, the largest tropical rainforest on the planet.

LUNGS OF THE PLANET

AMAZON BASIN, SOUTH AMERICA

The Amazon basin is one of the most diverse places for animals and plants in the world. Around 10 per cent of all the species we know about can be found there in that one habitat: 427 types of mammal, including jaguars, sloths and river dolphins; 1,300 species of bird, including harpy eagles, toucans, and macaw parrots; 378 varieties of reptile, including anacondas; and more than 400 species of amphibian, including poison dart frogs and glass frogs.

For thousands of years, the Amazon flourished. But in the last few decades, the Amazon has seen devastating changes. Many people have moved into the area to farm cattle for beef and leather, and to grow soy, as well as to export timber. More than 1.4 million hectares of forest have been razed to the ground since the 1970s; in the last few minutes, as you have been reading, thousands of trees in the rainforest have been cut down. Still more have been destroyed by fire. These fires, set deliberately, clear land so it can be used for farming.

The Amazon is also at risk because of climate change. If the planet continues to get hotter, the Amazon rainforest might eventually turn into a savannah. Not only would that wipe out the plants and animals that live there today, it would have grave consequences for the rest of us. That's because the Amazon rainforest plays a crucial role in cleaning the air we all breathe. There are around 390 billion trees in the Amazon, and each one takes harmful carbon dioxide out of the atmosphere and turns it into oxygen. That's why the rainforest is sometimes called 'The Lungs of the Planet'. If all the trees were destroyed, the amount of gas in the atmosphere that leads to global warming would vastly increase. Earth would heat up, and the world's weather would become more extreme.

It might feel like there is little you can do to protect the Amazon, but there are some ways you can help. Use less paper, recycle as much as you can, eat less beef and donate to charities that are trying to save the rainforest. The Amazon is essential to our survival and part of our world heritage. It is truly one of the most remarkable places on Earth.

TORTOISE SANCTUARY

ALDABRA, SEYCHELLES

Aldabra is a group of islands in the Seychelles, found in the Indian Ocean. It is surrounded by a pristine coral reef, which means it is very difficult to land a boat on the islands. They have largely been left untouched by humans.

As a result, the coral reefs are still in top condition and show us how abundant nature is when left to flourish without human interference and destruction. The lagoon of Aldabra teems with sharks, sea turtles and manta rays. To keep it safe far into the future, Aldabra has been made a nature reserve and very few people are allowed to visit it.

The islands are a haven for the Aldabra giant tortoise. There are 152,000 living on Aldabra, making it home to the world's largest population of these wonderful creatures. A long time ago, these tortoises would have roamed all over the islands of the Indian Ocean. But many of them were caught by hunters. Giant tortoises are easy to catch because they move slowly and because their heads

are too big to retreat into their shells. The tortoises don't have any natural predators so they didn't evolve ways to defend themselves, leaving them helpless in the face of hunters.

In the sixteenth century, people ate giant tortoises without a thought. Their oil was used to treat colds and cramps, and people loved to eat their eggs. They were also said to be convenient at sea, because they could be kept alive on boats for months without needing food or water. When giant tortoises drink, they can take in enough water to last them for months, storing it in a special bladder. Thirsty sailors could get supplies of fresh water out of the bladders of giant tortoises they had trapped on board. Thankfully, it is no longer acceptable to eat a tortoise for lunch and there are now more tortoises on the atoll than humans in the whole of the Seychelles!

This magnificent red rock gorge is totally overwhelming in size and beauty. Measuring 446 km long, 1.6 km deep and up to 29 km wide, it is hard to explain just how vast it really is. If you sit on its rim on a clear day, you can see for 160 km and take in the majesty and grandeur of the canyon.

The Grand Canyon began forming tens of millions of years ago, but was shaped into what we can see today by the Colorado river, which scientists think has been flowing through the area for five or six million years. The river still winds its way through the canyon, carving a path out of the rock, as it has done for millennia.

A RIVER MAKES ITS MARK

GRAND CANYON, USA

The river's path has exposed 40 layers of rock that took nearly two billion years to build up. These layers used to be underground but, thanks to the river, they are now out in the open. This allows geologists to learn about the formation of the Earth and how it has changed over time, because the Grand Canyon's walls are a record of history, showing when oceans came and went, mountains rose and fell, and deserts formed and disappeared. Fossils found in the rocks, including 500-million-year-old trilobites, scorpions and the wings of dragonflies, can tell us about the evolution of plants, amphibians, early mammals and even humans. It's a spectacular place to visit. The area around the Grand Canyon is teeming with interesting plants, birds and fish. Forest grows in parts of it, whilst other areas, by the bottom of the canyon, are baking hot desert. There are sandy beaches, waterfalls, hanging gardens and pools of water.

Native Americans have lived in the canyon for thousands of years, but the first European who is known to have seen it was a Spanish conquistador named Garcia López de Cardenas. He led an expedition in 1540, from what is now New Mexico, to find a river the local Hopi people had spoken of; it took the group 20 days to reach it. Hundreds of years later in 1869, John Wesley Powell, a geologist, became the first recorded person to lead a group of Europeans through the Grand Canyon. He and 10 men sailed on boats down the Colorado River; they had no idea what was around each corner because they were exploring uncharted land. The journey was hard work; 130 km into it, one crew lost control and their boat full of rations was smashed against the rocks. But Powell wasn't afraid; each afternoon he explored the sublime canyon, finding traces of people who had lived long before and marvelling at the ancient layers of the Earth. It was Powell who called it the Grand Canyon – the indigenous people of the area had their own names for it already: *Ongtupqa* in the Hopi tongue and *Tsékooh Hatsoh* in the Navajo.

It would be more than 100 years before anyone made the journey through the canyon on foot. Kenton Grua, a 25-year-old river guide, completed it in 1976 – that's 65 years after humans made it to the North and South Poles and 23 years after Tenzing Norgay and Edmund Hillary climbed to the summit of Mount Everest!

RAINFOREST OF THE OCEAN
GREAT BARRIER REEF, AUSTRALIA

The Great Barrier Reef is the world's largest living structure – and it's made entirely of coral. It runs for 2,300 km along the coast of eastern Australia, and is so big that if you stretched it out across Europe, it would reach from London to Moscow!

Coral may look like a piece of rock, but it is in fact made of tiny creatures called coral polyps. Each polyp has tentacles, a bottom, which they eat through, and a stomach. They also form a hard outer skeleton of limestone, which they attach to the dead skeletons of other polyps. Coral grows at a rate of 2.5 cm a year, creating reefs over millions of years.

Although coral polyps are see-through, the reefs have beautiful colours because of the colour of the algae that live on them. The algae live off waste products of the coral and the algae protect the reef from the harsh sunlight, turning it into their own energy source. Working together, coral and algae create reefs, which are like the rainforests of the ocean: they are home to a dazzling array of life including sponges, rays, dolphins, sea turtles and fish.

When the water around a reef gets too polluted or hot, the coral polyps expel the algae that live on them. Without it, the coral reef looks white. This is known as coral bleaching, and it's a big problem for the Great Barrier Reef. Huge sections of it are dying because global warming has warmed the ocean. Much of the coral in the northern sector of the reef died in 2016, when the sea was the hottest it had been since the year 1880. If the coral reef dies, everything in this beautiful, rich ecosystem will be lost as well.

Is there anything that can be done? Within Australia, it would help if farmers stopped using so much fertiliser, which can pollute the water. But everyone on the planet has a role to play. Whether growing our own food, using renewable energy or turning lights off when not needed, every small step towards a cleaner environment adds up – just as the work of each tiny coral polyp slowly creates a beautiful, pristine reef.

Have you ever heard the expression 'Lightning never strikes twice'? It's usually said when the speaker means 'Something really unusual happened, but it won't happen again'. Well, that might make for a nifty saying, but it's not actually true for lightning. It often strikes twice in the same place, and at the mouth of the Catatumbo river in Venezuela – the most electric place on Earth – it strikes in the same place up to 40,000 times a night.

EVERLASTING STORM

CATATUMBO LIGHTNING, VENEZUELA

For thousands of years, lightning has been striking the Catatumbo river where it meets Lake Maracaibo – it's known as the 'everlasting storm'. On average, electrical storms occur there 260 days of the year, and last for around nine hours each time. During the wet season, you can see 28 lightning flashes a second when a storm hits. It often rains and hails at the same time, so it's probably not the best place for a picnic!

Why is the area so electric? We don't know for sure, but it's probably because of the geography of the area and the local wind patterns. In the area where the electric storms happen, the mouth of the Catatumbo river is surrounded on one side by the Caribbean Sea and on the other three sides by the tall mountains of the Andes. The working theory goes something like this: during the day, water evaporates off the river and wind blows across the water, pushing warm air towards the mountains. At night, cold air filled with ice crystals tumbles from the mountains. The hot and cold air collide, creating tall storm clouds filled with electric charge. This energy is released as lightning, zigzagging down through the sky until it hits the ground.

What's so extraordinary about this phenomenon, known as Catatumbo lightning, is that it is a great source of ozone. Ozone is a special type of oxygen gas. 90 per cent of the planet's ozone is found in a layer of the atmosphere called the ozone layer, which protects life on Earth from the Sun's harmful radiation. Part of the ozone layer was destroyed by humans releasing too much pollution into the air. It's possible that the ozone gas created by the electric storms in Catatumbo is helping to mend the ozone layer, making life safer for all of us on Earth.

The largest ice cave in the world is called the Eisriesenwelt, also known as the World of the Ice Giants. It is part of a cave complex that stretches for more than 40 km below the Hochkogel Mountain on the outskirts of Salzburg, Austria. It is easy to imagine this underground labyrinth of caves, filled with frozen waterfalls and astonishing ice formations, being home to an ice giant or two.

LAND OF THE ICE GIANTS

EISRIESENWELT, AUSTRIA

The Eisriesenwelt is around 50 to 100 million years old. The cave was formed slowly over time by water erosion from the Salzach river; water seeped through limestone and dissolved it, creating large caves within the rock. The ice formed much more recently, around 1,000 years ago.

The strange shapes of the ice are created by air moving around inside the caves. In winter, the air inside the mountain is warmer than the air outside it: cold air moves into the passages of the cave and cools the lower part of the cave to below zero. In spring, melting water enters through cracks in the rock, and drips into cooler areas of the cave before freezing. This process creates amazing ice sculptures inside the mountain that change from season to season. This natural wonder is like a living work of art made of ice.

Austrian legend told that the Eisreisenwelt was the entrance to hell. The myth kept local people far away from the cave, fearing what would become of them if they stepped inside. But in 1879, an explorer called Anton von Posselt-Czorich walked 200 m into the cave and came back to tell the tale. From 1913, explorers and researchers set out to uncover the cave's mysteries.

Before long, the cave was also opened up to tourists. In the 1920s, paths to the cave were built, and today around 200,000 people go to see it each year. They can even take a cable car up to a mountain hut near the cave's entrance. If you're lucky enough to visit, wrap up warm and watch out for giants!

What a sight to behold: 100 million colourful, fragile butterflies flying for months in search of warmth and sunlight. Monarch butterflies are beautiful creatures with orange and black wings with white spots, which spend the summer months in North America. However, as the cold winter approaches, most of them set off on an epic 4,800-km journey to warmer climes.

THE FLUTTER OF 200 MILLION WINGS
MONARCH BUTTERFLY MIGRATION, NORTH AMERICA

The majority of the monarchs fly down to a tiny area in the mountains of Mexico. The rest – those that live west of the Rocky Mountain Range in the USA – migrate to a small selection of trees in southern California.

When they finally arrive in their winter sanctuaries, the monarchs huddle together, clinging to trees – called oyamel trees – in clusters that keep them warm and help them to survive. They look like bright orange and black hanging baskets in the trees. When the temperature warms up, the monarch butterflies fly all the way back again! If you stand in a skyscraper in Toronto, Canada, and look up at the right time of year, you will see them flying above you in their thousands.

The monarchs make this round trip every year and never get lost. Even though you or I would need a map to make such a long journey, the butterflies know where they're going. They have receptors in their eyes that can detect a special sort of light called UV, which is emitted from the Sun. By using the Sun to navigate, the butterflies fly straight to their destination, even though it takes them two months to complete the journey. What makes their navigation skills even more incredible is that they don't learn the way from their elders; the butterflies that migrate south each year have never been to Mexico.

No single butterfly ever makes the full journey. Monarch butterflies do not live for long, but they lay eggs during their travels. These turn into caterpillars and hatch into butterflies that carry on the journey, ensuring that monarch butterflies survive as a species. It takes four generations to make the round trip – the first three generations gradually fly down to Mexico and California, and the fourth generation flies all the way back!

Although there are millions of monarch butterflies, even some that do not migrate, humankind needs to help protect them. The monarchs who migrate need a very specific place to spend the winters; there are only around 12 mountaintops in Mexico that have the right environment for them to survive. These mountaintops need to stay free of roads, housing and farming so that the butterflies' habitat is protected.

We also need to safeguard the trees the butterflies fly to in southern California, such as eucalyptus trees, Monterey pines and Monterey cypresses, making sure they don't get cut down to make room for land developments. If we carefully protect the beautiful monarch butterflies in these ways, they will continue to thrive, flying back and forth as they chase the Sun.

Spring in Japan is a time of cherry blossom. Beautiful cherry trees in every town and city, and throughout the countryside, burst into beautiful pink and white bloom.

TRAIL OF BLOSSOM
SAKURA ZENSEN, JAPAN

Japan is a very long country made up of many islands, so spring arrives in the south first, and moves upwards to the north over a period of weeks. The cherry trees unfurl their blossoms to greet the spring sunshine, so they also bloom first in the south before moving north. This progression is called *sakura zensen*, meaning the 'cherry blossom front'.

Each year, newsreaders tell the public where the front has got to so they can plan trips to admire the blossom. During the few short days of bloom in each area, it is an annual tradition in Japan to sit beneath the pink and white blooms and share a picnic with family and friends to celebrate the flowers. This party is called *hanami*, which means 'flower viewing'.

> **"** For these few days, the hills are bright with cherry blossom. Longer, and we should not prize them so. **"**

Yamabe no Akahito, ancient Japanese poet

You can join in the Japanese tradition wherever you live, because cherry trees can be found in many places around the world. When spring arrives, see if you can find a tree in bloom – you might even feel like making a picnic to have a *hanami* party!

Way back in time – before maps existed, before humans were spread across the planet – the southern continents that we know today were once joined together as a super-continent. Its name was Gondwana, and the southern part of it was filled with a lush, verdant forest. Amazingly, some of that rainforest is still growing today.

PREHISTORIC FOREST

GONDWANA RAINFORESTS, AUSTRALIA

When the super-continent broke up into smaller pieces, a part on which the rainforest grew started drifting further south. That piece of land is now known as Australia, and parts of that prehistoric Gondwana rainforest can be found in the Australian states of Queensland and New South Wales. The Gondwana rainforests are filled with plants and animals that are almost identical to their ancient ancestors. Astonishingly, the vegetation that grows there today is directly linked to plants that grew over 100 million years ago. Much of it is very rare and found nowhere else on Earth, such as some of the world's oldest ferns and conifers.

The songbirds of the Gondwana rainforests are magnificent: you can see and hear lyrebirds, treecreepers and catbirds – not to mention bowerbirds, which are so named because the males make colourful nests, or bowers, filled with objects they find around the rainforest. The rainforests are so filled with life that species are still being discovered; two mammals that were thought to be extinct – the Hastings River mouse and Parma wallaby – have recently been found alive there.

When Australia separated from Gondwana, rainforest like this covered the continent for the next 40 million years. But the climate changed as Australia drifted into warmer parts of the planet, and much of the rainforest disappeared. By the time European settlers arrived in Australia in 1788, only 1 per cent of the continent was covered by rainforest; it was reduced even further when the new settlers cut down trees to make way for crops.

Today, only 0.25 per cent of the ancient rainforest remains. To ensure it is preserved for the future, the Gondwana rainforests have been given World Heritage status by the United Nations, meaning they will be protected by international treaties as well as by laws in their own country. Thank goodness the rainforests have been saved – how amazing it must be to stand under that canopy and know that you're seeing plants and animals that are almost the same as those which lived when all the continents on Earth were joined together.

The Great Blue Hole is a giant circle of deep blue, surrounded by aquamarine water. From the air, it looks like the giant pupil of an eye floating in the middle of the Caribbean Sea. For those lucky expert divers who are able to explore its true depths, the experience is unforgettable.

The Great Blue Hole is actually a huge, circular sinkhole under the water, measuring 145 m deep and 310 m wide. The hole is almost completely surrounded by a coral atoll called Lighthouse Reef, which teems with fish like wrasse and snapper.

THE EYE OF THE SEA
GREAT BLUE HOLE, BELIZE

The hole is such a dark colour because it is very deep – in striking contrast to the shallow sea washing over the pale coral of Lighthouse Reef. The sinkhole was once a huge limestone cave that began forming around 150,000 years ago. When the Ice Age ended, the water level of the sea rose and the cave flooded. Under the pressure of the water above it, the roof collapsed, leaving only the walls of the cave intact and forming an enormous submarine sinkhole.

The Great Blue Hole became famous when an underwater explorer named Jacques Yves-Cousteau declared it one of the top 10 dive sites in the world. Of course, plenty of people then wanted to go and see the astonishing geological feature themselves.

While there is much marine life to be seen near the surface of the reefs, such as anemones, angelfish, corals and purple seafans, the Great Blue Hole is so deep that divers won't see many sea creatures inside it. However, reef sharks and even the occasional hammerhead often pop by to say hello. Once you descend beyond 40 metres – the lowest depth that most recreational divers can reach – you'll find a cave filled with ancient stalactites and limestone formations. Eerily, you swim on, piercing the darkness with a waterproof torch, hearing only the sound of your own breathing and bubbles. In the cool, deep waters of the Great Blue Hole, it is easy to forget about the world above the sea.

Beneath the green hills of Waitomo, on the North Island of New Zealand, lies a labyrinth of caves, sinkholes and rivers carved by underground streams, pushing their way through the soft limestone over thousands of years. Overhead, the rocks are bathed in an ethereal glow.

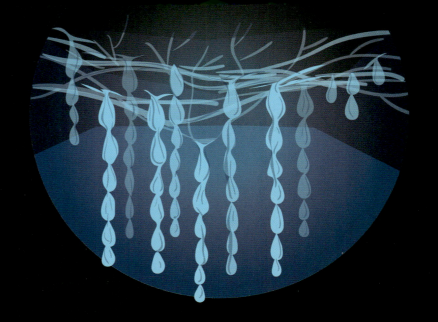

GLOWING CAVES

WAITOMO CAVES, NEW ZEALAND

Some of the caves have stalagmites growing up from the cave floor, and others have stalactites growing down. These are pointy cones of rock formed over centuries by dripping water. What makes the ones at Waitomo truly amazing is that they are lit up by a green-blue luminescent light generated by glow-worms that live on the roof and walls of the cave.

The glow-worms are the larvae of fungus gnats, just as caterpillars are the larvae of butterflies. Fungus gnats are little flies that feed on mushrooms. When the glow-worms hatch, they spin sticky strings of web from the roof of the cave. They drop blobs of mucus along the web strands, which makes them look like glass-bead necklaces hanging from the ceiling. Then the glow-worms hang from the threads and shine light from their tails.

Other creatures in the cave are attracted to the beads of light and move towards it – they can't see the sticky threads in the dark of the cave. Like moths to a flame, they fly into the web, where the glow-worms eat them.

Glow-worms use a chemical reaction called bioluminescence to make the light – plenty of creatures that dwell in dark places, such as the deep sea, use this clever technique to catch prey or to attract a mate. Insects, jellyfish, bacteria and even fungi all use bioluminescence.

The indigenous Māori people of New Zealand were first to discover the incredible Waitomo caves – the name comes from the Māori words *wai* (water) and *tomo* (hole). In the 1880s, a Māori chief named Tane Tinorau showed a British surveyor around; together, the two men entered the caves by sea on a raft, holding a burning torch aloft as they marvelled at the natural wonder. Tinorau later found an entrance on land, which is still used by visitors today. In 1889, the caves were opened to tourists, with local Māori showing them around. Even today, many of the guides who work there are descendants of Chief Tane Tinorau and his wife.

INDEX

A

Africa 22–23, 26, 30, 34–35
Aldabra giant tortoise 42
Aldabra 42
algae 38, 47
Amazon rainforest 41
Amazon river 41
amphibian 41, 44
anacondas 41
Anangu 29
Andes mountain range 10, 41, 48
Angola 22
animals 4, 5, 12, 18, 23, 26, 27, 29, 34, 37, 41, 57
Antarctica 15
anteaters 37
archipelago 12
Argentina 37
Armstrong, Neil 10
Atlantic Ocean 22, 41
aurora australis 16
aurora borealis 16
Australia 24, 28–9, 46–47, 57
aye-ayes 4, 34
Ayers Rock *see* Uluru

B

bacteria 18, 38
basalt 6
beach 12, 24, 25, 44
beavers 18
beetle 23
Belize 58
bioluminescence 25, 60
bird 4, 8–9, 27, 29, 37, 38, 39, 41, 44, 57
birds of paradise 4, 8–9
bison 18
black rhinos 26
blossom 5, 54–55
Bolivia 10–11
bowerbirds 57
Brazil 37, 41
broad-snouted caiman 37
buffalo 26
butterfly 4, 53

C

caiman 37
California 32, 53
canyon 18, 44
Cape fur seals 30
Cape Town, South Africa 30
carbon dioxide 5, 11, 41
Cardenas, Garcia López de 44
Caribbean Sea 48, 58

Catatumbo lightning 48
Catatumbo river 48
cattle 27, 41
cave 4, 6, 21, 50, 59, 60
Cave of Crystals 21
cheetahs 26
cherry blossom 54–55
cherry trees 54–55
Chihuahua, Mexico 21
chinstrap penguins 15
Christmas Island 24
cinnabar 12
climate change 23, 32, 41
Colorado river 44
conquistador 44
coral 4, 42, 46–47, 58–59
coyotes 18
crabs 24, 35
cradle of mankind 26
crystals 21, 48

D

Darwin, Charles 12
deforestation 37
desert 4, 12, 22–23, 29, 44
desert elephants 23
desert rose 12
Devil's Throat 37
divers 58–59
dolphins 41, 47
dragon's blood tree 4, 12
Dreamtime 29

E

eagle 27, 37, 41
eggs 24, 38, 39, 43, 53
Eisriesenwelt 50
electrical storm 48
elephants 23, 26
elk 18
endemic 12, 34
erosion 50

F

falcons 27
fever trees 26
fig trees 26
Fingal's Cave 6
firefly squid 25
flamingo 27, 38, 39
fog 22–23
forest 18, 24, 26, 27, 32, 35, 41, 44, 57
fossil fuels 5, 11
fossils 32, 44
foxes 18
frogs 35, 41
fungus gnats 60

G

Galápagos 12
Galilei, Galileo 16
Garganta del Diablo, la 37

gecko 23
General Sherman 32
genes 12
geyser 18
giant anteaters 37
Giant Forest 32
giant sequoia 4, 32
giant tortoise 4, 42–43
Giant's Causeway 6
glass frogs 41
global warming 5, 41, 47
glow-worms 60
Gondwana 57
gorge 44
Grand Canyon 18, 44
Grand Prismatic Spring 18
Great Barrier Reef 4, 46–47
Great Blue Hole 58–59
Great Rift Valley 26–27
great white sharks 30
greater bird of paradise 9
grizzly bears 18
Grua, Kenton 44

H

hanami 54, 55
hanging gardens 44
harpy eagle 37, 41
Hartmann's mountain zebras 23
Hastings River mouse 57
hedgehog tenrec 35
Hochkogel mountain 50
Hopi 44
hot springs 18, 38

I

ice 48, 50
ice cave 50
Iguazú Falls 37
Iguazú National Park 37
Iguazú river 37
Indian Ocean 12, 34, 42
Indri Lemur 34
inselberg 29
Ireland 6
island 4, 6, 8, 12, 15, 24, 28, 30, 34, 38, 39, 42, 54, 60

J

jaguar 37, 41
Japan 25, 54–55

K

Kavango-Zambezi Transfrontier Conservation Area (KAZA) 23
king bird of paradise 8

L

Lago Minchín 10
lake 10, 18, 38–39, 48
Lake Maracaibo 48
Lake Natron 38–39

lemur 4, 34
leopards 26
lesser flamingo 38, 39
Lighthouse Reef 58–59
lightning 48
lions 26
lithium 11
logging 37
Lucy 27

M
Maasai 27
macaroni penguins 15
macaw parrots 41
Madagascar 4, 34–35
mammal 35, 41, 44, 57
manta rays 24, 42
Māori 60
McCool, Finn 6
Mendelssohn, Felix 6
Mexico 21, 53
migration 24, 53
mineral 21, 28–29, 38
monarch butterfly 53
mountain 4, 10, 18, 21, 28–29, 32, 44, 48, 50, 53

N
Namib Desert 22–23
Namib Desert beetle 23
Namibia 22–23, 30
national park 18, 37
Native Americans 44
natural selection 12
nature reserve 26, 42
Navajo 44
New Guinea 8
New Zealand 60
Ngorongoro Crater 26–27
North America 18, 53
North pole 16
Northern Lights 16
Noxious Bluff, Zavodovski Island 15

O
ocelots 37
ostriches 27
oyamel trees 53
ozone 48

P
Pacific Ocean 8
Parana Plateau 37
Parma wallaby 57
parrots 41
penguins 15
Peru 41
Petermanns 28
plains 26
plants 4, 12, 26, 29, 34, 37, 41, 44, 57
poison dart frogs 41
pollution 48

polyps 46–47
ponds 26
Posselt-Czorich, Anton von 50
Powell, John Wesley 44
primate 34
Pungent Point, Zavodovski Island 15
pygmy mouse lemur 34

R
rabbits 18
rainforest 4, 37, 41, 46–47, 57
rays 24, 42, 47
red land crabs 24
reef 4, 42, 46–47, 58–59
renewable energy 5, 11, 47
reptile 41
rhinos 26
Ring of Death 30
river 18, 26, 37, 41, 44, 48, 50, 60
river dolphins 41

S
sakura zensen 54
Salar de Uyuni 10–11
salt 10–11, 21
salt flat 10–11
Salzach river 50
savannah 41
Scotland 6
sea turtles 42, 47
Seal Island 30
seals 30
Seneca 16
sequoia 4, 32
Seychelles 42
sharks 24, 30, 42
Sierra Nevada mountain range 32
sinkhole 58–59, 60
Skeleton Coast 23
sloths 41
Socotra 12, 34
Socotran desert rose 12
solar wind 16
songlines 29
South Africa 22, 30
South America 12, 41
South pole 16
South Sandwich Islands 15
Southern Lights 16
soy 41
spirulina 38
sponges 47
spring 25, 32, 50, 54, 55
squid 24–25
Staffa, Scotland 6
storks 27
storm 48
summer 10, 53
superb bird of paradise 8
supervolcano 26
swamps 41

T
Tanzania 26, 38
tenrec 4, 35
timber 41
Tinorau, Tane 60
tortoise 4, 42–43
toucans 37, 41
Toyama Bay, Japan 25
trees 4, 5, 12, 18, 24, 26, 27, 32, 34, 37, 41, 53, 54–55, 57
turtles 42, 47

U
Uluru 28–29
USA 18, 21, 32, 44, 53

V
Venezuela 48
volcanic springs 18
volcano 6, 15, 18, 21, 26

W
Waitomo Caves 60
waterfall 18, 37, 44, 50
weasels 18
web-footed gecko 23
web-footed tenrec 35
whale sharks 24
wildebeest 26
wildlife 12, 23, 27, 34
winter 10, 50, 53
wolves 18
World of the Ice Giants 50

Y
Yellowstone National Park 18
Yemen 12
Yves-Cousteau, Jacques 59

Z
Zavodovski Island, South Sandwich Islands 15
zebra 23

For Mama
and for A, my favourite natural wonder of the world
xxx – M.O.

First published in Great Britain in 2019 by Wren & Rook

Text © Molly Oldfield, 2019
Illustrations © Federica Bordoni, 2019
Design © Hodder & Stoughton Limited, 2019
All rights reserved.

ISBN: 978 1 5263 6066 3
E-book ISBN: 978 1 5263 6067 0
10 9 8 7 6 5 4 3 2 1

Wren & Rook
An imprint of
Hachette Children's Group
Part of Hodder & Stoughton
Carmelite House
50 Victoria Embankment
London EC4Y 0DZ

An Hachette UK Company
www.hachette.co.uk
www.hachettechildrens.co.uk

Publishing Director: Debbie Foy
Senior Editor: Liza Miller
Art Director: Laura Hambleton
Designer: Anna Lubecka

Printed in China

Picture acknowledgements:
The publisher would like to thank the following for permission to reproduce their pictures:
p 6-7 Alan Payton / Alamy Stock Photo; p 9 szefei / iStock; p 10-11 ShantiHesse / iStock; p 13 Anton_Ivanov / Shutterstock.com; p 14-15 mzphoto11 / iStock; p 16-17 Nick_Pandevonium / iStock; p 18-19 Kris Wiktor / Shutterstock.com; p 20 Carsten Peter/Speleoresearch & Films / Getty Images; p 22-23 Paul & Paveena Mckenzie / Getty Images; p 24 Nature Picture Library / Alamy Stock Photo; p 25 Nature Picture Library / Alamy Stock Photo; p 26-27 Travel Stock / Shutterstock.com; p 28-29 Maurizio De Mattei / Shutterstock.com; p 30-31 Imageplotter / Alamy Stock Photo; p 32-33 welcomia / Shutterstock.com; p 34 (top) blickwinkel / Alamy Stock Photo; p 34 (bottom) imageBROKER / Alamy Stock Photo; p 35 Ryan M. Bolton / Shutterstock.com; p 36-37 mytrade1 / iStock; p 38-39 Minden Pictures / Alamy Stock Photo; p 40 Will & Deni McIntyre / Getty Images; p 42-43 Thomas P. Peschak / Getty Images; p 44-45 kojhirano / iStock; p 46-47 Marco Brivio / Getty Images; p 48-49 © Alan Highton; p 50-51 National Geographic Creative / Alamy Stock Photo; p 52 Ingo Arndt/Minden Pictures / Alamy Stock Photo; p 54-55 jiratto / Shutterstock.com; p 56 B.G. Thomson / Science Photo Library; p 58-59 Matteo Colombo / Getty Images; p. 61 Marcel Strelow / Alamy Stock Photo.

Every effort has been made to clear copyright. Should there be any inadvertent omission, please apply to the publisher for rectification.

The website addresses (URLs) included in this book were valid at the time of going to press. However, it is possible that contents or addresses may have changed since the publication of this book. No responsibility for any such changes can be accepted by either the author or the publisher.